THE ROOT CAUSE ANALYSIS OF A BALANCED LEADER

Phil Ford, MSM
Michael Blisko, MHA

authorHOUSE®

AuthorHouse™
1663 Liberty Drive
Bloomington, IN 47403
www.authorhouse.com
Phone: 1 (800) 839-8640

Published by AuthorHouse 01/15/2015

ISBN: 978-1-5049-7000-6 (sc)
ISBN: 978-1-5049-7001-3 (hc)
ISBN: 978-1-5049-6999-4 (e)

Library of Congress Control Number: 2016900253

Print information available on the last page.

This book is printed on acid-free paper.

THE RCA OF A BALANCED LEADER

Table of Contents

THE RCA OF A
BALANCED LEADER

THE RCA OF A BALANCED LEADER

SPECIAL NOTE TO THE READER

You will find this book to be quite unique. It is printed for the reader in a presentation format. Starting with the next page, the reader will find a two-page offering with the page to the left representing a presentation slide and the page to the right the narrative discussion of that slide.

THE RCA OF A BALANCED LEADER

Personal Growth Model

Socrates: "The unexamined life is not worth living."

THE RCA OF A BALANCED LEADER

Socrates: "The unexamined life is not worth living."

A Balanced Leader. A term that could mean many things.

Many years ago, I answered the questions in one of those scientific studies which was designed to help determine what category of perceived management styles I fit into. It was the one where results were placed on a graph above or below the zero axis. The facilitator explained that of the four identified points being graphed, those above the zero axis were the dominant, and those below the zero axis were present, but not dominant.

Well, all four of my points were scored on the graph above the zero axis. The facilitator said that was rare. She continued to say that tended to mean I was trying to be all things to all people at all times. She added that must be incredible stressful!

Well, welcome to Contemporary Leadership! This is where it is a natural expectation to be all things to all people at all times. You just have to determine the who, what, when, where, how and why of your current position, within your current set of circumstances. That determination will assist you in being the most effective leader you can be, at the most appropriate time, and assist those you lead in becoming the most productive people they can be.

The question is not are you a leader? The assumption for those reading or taking part in a presentation is that you are already in leadership roles. The question is rather what kind of leader are you and how can you become a better leader?

To that end, let's begin the process of examination. Socrates was quoted as saying, "The unexamined life is not worth living." One of the most critical thinkers in Earth's recorded history puts a very fine point on this issue – words are not minced; there is no duality in the message; there is no gray area to the meaning. To have a life worth living, one must examine the fundamental elements of that life.

THE RCA OF A BALANCED LEADER

Personal Growth Model

Socrates: "The unexamined life is not worth living."

Thomas Edison: "Show me a thoroughly satisfied man, and I will show you a failure."

THE RCA OF A
BALANCED LEADER

Thomas Edison: "Show me a thoroughly satisfied man, and I will show you a failure."

"I'm done."

"There's nothing more to do."

"I can see no way to improve this."

"It's the way it's always been done."

"Anything worth inventing has already been invented," or so said the stuffy Science Academy Minister in the movie Around the World in Eighty Days.

Satisfaction is a good thing. To reach a point where you have achieved pre-set goals is a great feeling. But, Edison stresses the point that we should be concerned if we find ourselves thoroughly satisfied - all categories, at all levels.

It happens to some people. They're tired, worn-out, and believe they have not only given their all, but that they have no more to give.

Remember the Big Dog slogan that stated the view only changes for the Lead Dog?

Well, consider this: Love the View or Accept the Dust!

Personal Growth Model

Socrates: "The unexamined life is not worth living."

Thomas Edison: "Show me a thoroughly satisfied man, and I will show you a failure."

It's been said, nothing is perfect. Then, there is always room for improvement!

THE RCA OF A BALANCED LEADER

It's been said, nothing is perfect.

The phrase, "nothing is perfect," is often taken to mean since there is no perfection, we cannot possibly be expected to achieve perfection. But what about the other meaning of nothing is perfect?

What if it truly says to us that since nothing is perfect, then there is always room for improvement!

If your business is under producing, running at a loss, with the bill collectors knocking at your doors, and you've determined that each and every one of your systems is operating as it should with no room for improvement, then you're in a bad place.

But, if you've determined that some of your systems have room for improvement, then you have just given your business, and yourself, hope. Finding the system flaws or failures provides you with a chance to improve, to grow, and to better produce thus reaching or even exceeding your goals.

Personal Growth Model

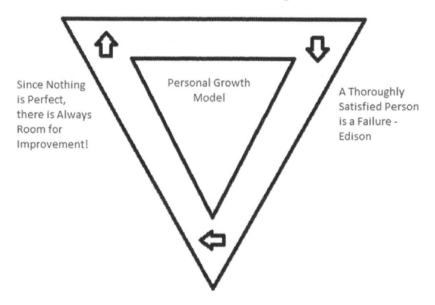

The Unexamined Life is not Worth Living - Socrates

Since Nothing is Perfect, there is Always Room for Improvement!

Personal Growth Model

A Thoroughly Satisfied Person is a Failure - Edison

THE RCA OF A BALANCED LEADER

Personal Growth Model

> Socrates: "The unexamined Life is not worth Living."
>
> Thomas Edison: "Show me a thoroughly satisfied man, and I will show you a failure."
>
> It's been said, nothing is perfect. Nothing is perfect is often taken to mean that since there is no perfection, then we cannot be expected to achieve perfection. But what about the other meaning of nothing is perfect? What if it truly says to us that if nothing is perfect, then there is always room for improvement!

So, as Leaders, you must regularly perform a process of self- examination to establish an understanding of who you are in this particular life-role. To become a better leader, you must first understand YOU. Once you have a working understanding of who you are as a leader, then you will be able to use that understanding to fuel the support, guidance, and urging necessary to productively and effectively ignite others to action.

This process of study and self-analysis can be logically assisted through the use of a derivative of the Socratic Method, by exercising an inquiry that is based on asking and answering questions to stimulate critical thinking and to illuminate ideas. Much of this examination will utilize aspects from the field of Healthcare, even though many of the attributes, theories, and eventual discoveries about the Leaders easily convey to any area of Leadership.

Personal Growth Model

Socrates: "The unexamined life is not worth living."

Thomas Edison: "Show me a thoroughly satisfied man, and I will show you a failure."

It's been said, nothing is perfect. Then, there is always room for improvement!

A flawed diamond is more valuable than a perfect chunk of coal.

THE RCA OF A BALANCED LEADER

It's been said by many people, A flawed diamond is more valuable than a perfect chunk of coal.

Many situations we encounter as Leaders in healthcare relate to that comment. Consider census for a moment. Let's say you're running a pretty good building, but your census is below expectations. With census below expectations, your ability to meet other financial expectations becomes problematic.

So, you examine your overall plan to improve your census. You study materials used, the people in place and the activities performed by the people. If you examine all of these aspects and find no room for improvement – all aspects being performed at their optimal level – then you have yourself a perfect chunk of coal. No flaws and not worth much.

Conversely, your examination might discover aspects that have not been executed well, or as well as they could have been. You may find that the people in place are not well aligned with the goals – they either could benefit from additional training or should be reassigned or replaced. Your examination may identify the need to adjust the materials being used or the need to alter advertising approaches.

If your census is below expectations and you discover viable possibilities to alter your efforts for improving census, then you have discovered a potentially flawed diamond – worth much more than the perfect chunk of coal because it still provides you with the possibility of success after identifying the existing flaws.

THE RCA OF A BALANCED LEADER

On or In your Game

You must be On your Game to be In your Game

Question ourselves regularly to make sure we are keeping our eyes on the right targets (Goals).

THE RCA OF A BALANCED LEADER

You must be On your Game to be In your Game

Question ourselves regularly to make sure we are keeping our eyes on the right targets (Goals).

The other evening I was talking with someone who was questioning their ability to perform their job at the high level at which they were used to performing.
During this conversation, I pointed out   that YOU HAVE TO BE ON IT IF YOU WANT TO BE IN IT.

What does that mean? You must "be on you game" if you want to "be in the game."

Consider these three points:

1. We need to question ourselves regularly to make sure we are keeping our eyes on the right targets (goals).

2. We need to examine our systems to make sure they are functioning in the manner we intend (plays).

3. We need to practice our behaviors enough to make sure they are first nature to us (execution). Did you realize we are paid more for the practice time than we are for the success time? Think about it. There's a lot more practice time than there is game or success time. We are paid to practice.

We need to question ourselves regularly to make sure we are keeping our eyes on the right targets. What are you aiming at? Why have you chosen that goal? How often do you prioritize your goals? Do you expect to hit your target – your goal – accidently? Be intentional about the pursuit of your goals. Make sure you have committed yourself fully to the pursuit of your chosen goals.

Whatever you do, Be there when you do it!

THE RCA OF A BALANCED LEADER

On or In your Game

You must be On your Game to be In your Game

Question ourselves regularly to make sure we are keeping our eyes on the right targets (Goals).

Examine our systems to make sure they are functioning in the manner we intend (Plays).

Examine our systems to make sure they are functioning in the manner we intend (Plays).

You've chosen and confirmed your goals. Now, you need a system in place to pursue those goals – you need plays.

In football, your current short term goal could be to achieve a first down by moving the ball an additional five yards. You have a running play you believe gives you the best chance to obtain your goal and gain those five yards. To perform this play most productively, you need to have some of your players push a couple of the defensive linemen to one direction to create a gap that your running back can run through to gain those five yards.

You also have determined that you need some of your players to create a diversion on the opposite side of the line from the point you want your running back to pierce the created gap. In addition, you want further diversion from the running back, so you have a couple of the receivers take off down the field like you plan to throw them the ball.

The results of your play? If your system's elements functioned as planned and created the right two diversions by pushing the defensive linemen apart just enough for your running back to pierce the gap and gain the needed five yards, the result will be a first down and an extended opportunity earned to score points.

You need systems in place to achieve your goals.

On or In your Game

You must be On your Game to be In your Game

Question ourselves regularly to make sure we are keeping our eyes on the right targets (Goals).

Examine our systems to make sure they are functioning in the manner we intend (Plays).

Practice our behaviors enough to make sure they are first nature to us (Execution).

THE RCA OF A BALANCED LEADER

Practice our behaviors enough to make sure they are first nature to us (Execution).

How old is the phrase, "practice makes perfect?"

What about the line from the movie *The Last Action Hero* that asks, "How do you get to Carnegie Hall? Practice – practice – practice."

I heard an interview with the former Colt and future NFL Hall of Fame wide receiver, Marvin Harrison, questioning him about his view of practice. He said he believed he was paid to practice and got to play in the games for fun.

You have a goal – a target. Then you have systems or plays in place to acquire that goal and hit that target. Now you practice those behaviors so they become so natural they are first nature to you.

This represents the Successful Execution of the Plan.

On or In your Game

You must be On your Game to be In your Game

Question ourselves regularly to make sure we are keeping our eyes on the right targets (Goals).

Examine our systems to make sure they are functioning in the manner we intend (Plays).

Practice our behaviors enough to make sure they are first nature to us (Execution).

You have to be ON IT if you want to be IN IT!

THE RCA OF A BALANCED LEADER

You have to be ON IT if you want to be IN IT!

You have to be on your game – succeeding at these three points-

1 - Question ourselves regularly to make sure we are keeping our eyes on the right targets (Goals);

2 - Examine our systems to make sure they are functioning in the manner we intend (Plays);

3 - Practice our behaviors enough to make sure they are first nature to us (Execution);

– in order to be in the game.

Don't be sidelined by your mistakes or failures. Select your goals, implement the needed systems of success and then execute your plan through Practice – Practice – Practice.

People can be divided into three groups:

1. Those who make things happen

People can be divided into three groups:

1. Those who make things happen

You know what you want.

You go after it with energy and focus. You push people's buttons until you see the results you're after.

You make things happen!

People can be divided into three groups:

1. Those who make things happen

2. Those who watch things happen

2. Those who watch things happen

You appreciate the activity going on around you.

You feel you are busy because of the activity going on around you.

Sometimes, you share in the success of others because of the activity they engineered and you were swept-up by.

You watch things happen.

People can be divided into three groups:

1. Those who make things happen

2. Those who watch things happen

3. Those who wonder what's happening

3. Those who wonder what's happening

You aren't quite sure what the goals are.

You aren't quite sure who's responsible for achieving those goals.

You aren't quite sure who set the goals or why.

You aren't quite sure of lot of things, but you do know you don't want to rock the boat.

You just wonder what's happening.

Practice

With Practice, success is a first time caller, first time visitor, something new.

THE RCA OF A
BALANCED LEADER

With Practice, success is a first time caller, first time visitor, something new.

We talked earlier about the importance of practice.

Practice starts somewhere. You had an itch to get something done or make something better. From that initial itch, you began practicing a more successful behavior. That successful behavior honed and better tuned your efforts to the point that you achieved your first success as a result of the newly practiced behavior.

Success was a first time caller, first time visitor; something new.

Practice

With Practice, success is a first time caller, first time visitor, something new.

After Continued Practice, the caller becomes a guest, a regular visitor with whom you are becoming more familiar.

THE RCA OF A
BALANCED LEADER

After Continued Practice, the caller becomes a guest, a regular visitor with whom you are becoming more familiar.

That first time caller success felt good.

That initial itch felt good to be satisfied. So, you continue this newly acquired behavior.

As you keep practicing, you become more comfortable with the new behavior. It feels less foreign to you as you exercise it.

After continued practice, the caller becomes a guest, a regular visitor with whom you are becoming more familiar.

Practice

With Practice, success is a first time caller, first time visitor, something new.

After Continued Practice, the caller becomes a guest, a regular visitor with whom you are becoming more familiar.

Finally, with continued, consistent Practice, success is so natural it becomes the master.

Finally, with continued, consistent Practice, success is so natural it becomes the master.

Starting with the scratching of that initial itch, you seem to achieve success much easier now. The behavior is not only less foreign, but the familiarity with this behavior has achieved a newly attained comfort level.

It seems so natural now to employ this behavior. You don't even have to think about it. R e l a t e d circumstances arise and the behavior activates. At one time, you had to cognitively decide that was the behavior to enact. Then, with continued practice, you gave the familiar behavior merely a quick review.

Now, with continued, consistent practice, success is so natural it becomes the master.

THE RCA OF A
BALANCED LEADER

Practice

With Practice, success is a first time caller, first time visitor, something new.

After Continued Practice, the caller becomes a guest, a regular visitor with whom you are becoming more familiar.

Finally, with continued, consistent Practice, success is so natural it becomes the master...

Maybe the Secret of Success is to start
from scratch, and then keep scratchin!

THE RCA OF A
BALANCED LEADER

So, maybe the Secret of Success is to Start from Scratch, and then Keep Scratchin!

SUCCESS MODEL

Examination leads to Discovery

THE RCA OF A
BALANCED LEADER

Examination leads to discovery.

Success, what does it mean? We throw the word around all the time and use it in uncounted opportunities to describe our achievements.

Webster's Dictionary says that Success is "the favorable or prosperous termination of attempts or endeavors; the accomplishment of one's goals."

I knew a Healthcare Administrator who shared with me he had been in his position for five years and during that five years, he had employed and lost seven Directors of Nursing. What he discovered through his initial examination was his Facility had been hindered greatly by this inordinately high Director of Nursing (DON) turnover rate. The Facility could not grow and mature due to the lack of consistency at this key DON position.

SUCCESS MODEL

Examination leads to Discovery

Discovery leads to Understanding

THE RCA OF A BALANCED LEADER

Discovery leads to understanding.

Identifying this reality that his facility could not grow with the DON position in constant turmoil, this Administrator asked for my help in recruiting. As we were in the midst of discussing the problem, I asked the Administrator if he had considered the causes for the turnover? He began sharing the various reasons the outgoing DONs had expressed as they resigned. None of the reasons seemed to repeat themselves except the outgoing DONs were never able to truly get control of their Nursing Department.

With this identified common statement in mind, the Administrator and I began discussing reasons why a DON might not be able to gain control of their department. At the end of this brainstorming session, I asked the Administrator a direct question. "What is the one constant that stands out during this five year, seven DON period of time?" The Administrator had a blank expression – he had no clear idea.

I continued, "You; you are the constant." The Administrator became defensive at first. He started describing how hard he worked. How many hours he put in. How the Residents, their families and the facility staff have always felt comfortable coming to him, with anything, knowing that he would address their issues. With that, the Administrator went silent.

I stayed quiet for a moment as well. The Administrator spoke first, asking me, "What is it you always say? The main reason a staff member breaks chain of command is because they are allowed, and sometimes encouraged, to do so. I think that's what I've done. I have not allowed my DONs to lead their department because I always intervened and led the department instead."

"Wow, I was the constant."

SUCCESS MODEL

Examination leads to Discovery

Discovery leads to Understanding

Understanding leads to putting into Practice what you
have learned

THE RCA OF A
BALANCED LEADER

Understanding leads to putting into practice what you have learned.

So, the Administrator endeavored to learn from that realization.

It was very difficult for the Administrator at first. You may accept you have control of your actions, but habits are hard to break. Day in and day out, for the first ninety days of his newest DON's tenure, this Administrator struggled with not answering for his DON. He began redirecting questions appropriate for the DON to address to the DON. Staff, at first, balked at the Administrator's new response to their questions. In time though, they began taking those questions directly to the DON giving her a chance to earn their trust and respect.

SUCCESS MODEL

Examination leads to Discovery

Discovery leads to Understanding

Understanding leads to putting into Practice what you have learned

Practice leads to Success

THE RCA OF A BALANCED LEADER

Practice leads to Success

The Administrator has now stopped constantly turning over his DON position. The DON he hired and began his journey of change with had been in that Facility as their DON for over four years at the time this book was published.

Through Examination of his DON turnover, leading to the Discovery that he was more than likely the cause of the DON turnover, followed by his putting his Understanding to the test by Practicing new behaviors in his relationship with his staff and his DON, this Administrator finally achieved a well- earned level of success.

Practice leads to Success.

Success Model

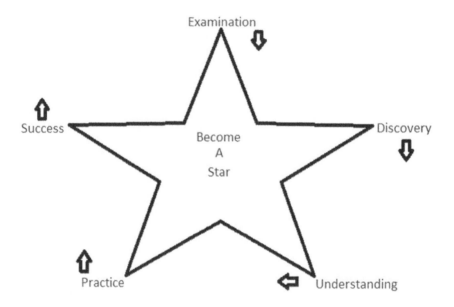

THE RCA OF A BALANCED LEADER

Let's Begin the Examination ---

Acquired Understanding Model

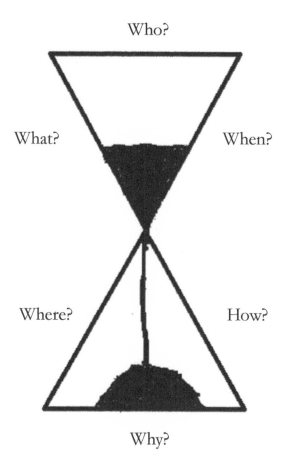

Who?

What?   When?

Where?   How?

Why?

The Acquired Understanding Model represents elements of time passing within a structure of discovery. The process of asking questions – examination – takes time. You cannot hurry or rush the process and remain effective.

Each step in the process takes time as well. Each question asked must go through the process. This takes time.

So, the time needed for these processes is represented by the hourglass and the movement of The Sands of Time. The motion required is represented by the asking of the questions.

The length of time required for each step in the process, of course, differs with each individual. A skipped step will create a hole in the discovery process. If the issue missed as a result of skipping a step in the process is of large enough magnitude, the hole in the discovery process might best be represented by the properties of a Singularity, also known as a Black Hole, which could completely disrupt any project.

Acquired Understanding Model

Who?

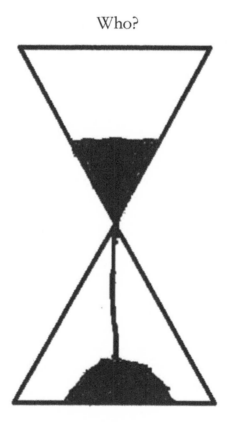

THE RCA OF A
BALANCED LEADER

Acquired Understanding Model – Who?

WHO

Who are you leading?

Have you ever wondered why
there are so few Absolutes?

THE RCA OF A
BALANCED LEADER

Have you ever wondered why there are so few absolutes?

Hardly ever do we operate in a situation where "always" or "never" truthfully rule the day. Perhaps it's because people are "always" the variable. You don't lead the same people all of the time. Faces and names change from time to time. Also, even if the people's faces and names don't change, the same people change over time.

In the Health Care arena, there are obvious and not so obvious groups and individuals being led. How well do you know those groups? What makes them happy; sad; upset? Examining those groups should help shed light on you as a Leader.

Understanding these variables and continuously positioning them in the forefront of your mind will assist you in leading your team, keeping them and you focused on your Mission.

WHO

Who are you leading?

Have you ever wondered why
there are so few Absolutes?

1. Staff

THE RCA OF A BALANCED LEADER

Staff

First, and most obvious, you have a staff of employees you lead. These people come to their various positions with backgrounds of education and training making them appropriate for their job descriptions. Some are college educated with specific degrees in nursing, business, dietetics, recreational therapy, and social work, while still others have degrees in areas unrelated to the job they have accepted. Some of these individuals sought their current positions throughout their collegiate experience. Some fell into their positions accidentally choosing their current health care profession for reasons other than their collegiate goals.

You also lead staff members who may have no formal college-level education. They have learned by doing. Their ability to successfully perform their specific job is predicated upon the accumulated results of their job training, and as such their being taught by others who served as their mentors. Assumptions may be made about the quality of either of these learning paths, but the proof is in their performance.

A Leader should not only consider their staff's educational backgrounds, but those you lead also come to you with a multitude of personal backgrounds. Some have been in their fields for a number of years – some are fairly new, if not brand new, at what they do. Some are married with children, while some are still single or married with no children. Some come to you with family structures that support their career efforts, while some must strive with their families over their choice of employment. Some come into your employment arena directly, while some have tried several career choices prior to placing themselves with you.

You, as a Leader, must work to understand these foundations which worked to spring-board your staff into their current areas of responsibility.

WHO

Who are you leading?

Have you ever wondered why
there are so few Absolutes?

1. Staff

2. Residents

THE RCA OF A BALANCED LEADER

Residents

In the health care arena, you as a Leader are also responsible to lead a group of residents. Without the existence of residents you would have nothing to lead in the health care field. So who are the residents you lead?

They come to you in need. Some of your residents have acute needs with the potential of being addressed, alleviated and possibly resolved. While other residents come to you with chronic needs that may place them in your care for the balance of their lives. Not only their clinical, but their psycho- social needs are brought to you as well.

These residents come to you with varied backgrounds as well. They are of different ages. They are of different educational and cultural backgrounds.

WHO

Who are you leading?

Have you ever wondered why
there are so few Absolutes?

1. Staff

2. Residents

3. Families

THE RCA OF A BALANCED LEADER

Families

Most of the residents you provide care to also have families and friends who must be guided through this process. One cannot provide care in a vacuum. Relatives play an active part in the care received by your residents. How the care is received by your residents is often affected by the relationship you have with those relatives. This is often overlooked, but is a strong, realistic force with many overlapping areas in daily leadership.

There are families with varied backgrounds and expectations:

> Expectations – perceived, voiced, realistic, unrealistic
>
> Involvement – all levels from not at all to daily
>
> The Family's Psycho Social needs – often greater than the resident's.

WHO

Who are you leading?

Have you ever wondered why
there are so few Absolutes?

1. Staff

2. Residents

3. Families

4. Physicians

Physicians

Residents either come with their own physicians, or they are introduced to a new group of physicians as they enter your care environment. Physicians too are led through the process by you.

Physicians with varied specialties and limitations:

> Medical Director
>
> Individual MDs – Primary Care Physicians, Specialty Physicians
>
> MDs who perform their facility visits on their own
>
> MDs who want one of your nurses to assist them
>
> MDs with Nurse Practitioner support
>
> MDs with no on-call physician back-up

WHO

Who are you leading?

Have you ever wondered why there are so few Absolutes?

1. Staff

2. Residents

3. Families

4. Physicians

5. Ancillary Providers

THE RCA OF A
BALANCED LEADER

Ancillary Providers

Your residents are more than likely affected by others in the healthcare spectrum as well. Ancillary providers such as pharmacies, dialysis centers, various supply vendors, etc., are a part of the provision of care to your residents. You are the leader responsible to guide these entities in a successful manner conducive to meeting the needs of your residents.

Ancillary healthcare providers with varied services and goals:

      Pharmacy

      Therapy

      Hospice

      Food Suppliers

      Med Supplies

      Physical Plant Support

WHO

Who are you leading?

Have you ever wondered why there are so few Absolutes?

1. Staff

2. Residents

3. Families

4. Physicians

5. Ancillary Providers

6. A Community of Citizens

A Community of Citizens

You may think this description has covered the various groups or individuals you lead in your career life, but this is not the case. At least one additional, rather large group is affected by your leadership in this arena - your Community at large.

A Community of citizens with varied goals of their own:

Local Public Relations

Local Government

Your building's neighbors

Local vendors

Regulatory Entities

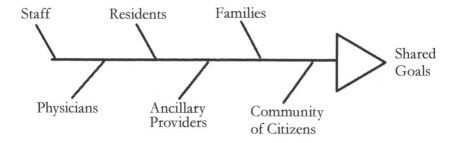

**THE RCA OF A
BALANCED LEADER**

Staff   Residents   Families

Shared
Goals

Physicians   Ancillary
Providers   Community
of Citizens

THE RCA OF A BALANCED LEADER

Shared Goals Model

The Shared Goals Model represents how each of these groups are tied together, with you as their Leader, on a journey towards specific and Shared Goals.

Leader's Style Model

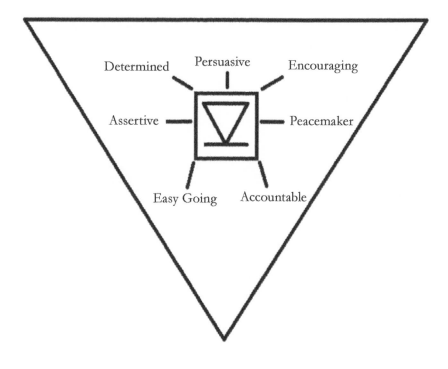

Who are you as you lead?

LEADER'S STYLE MODEL

Who are you as you lead?

LEADER'S STYLE MODEL

1. Accountable

THE RCA OF A BALANCED LEADER

Are you Accountable? According to *Webster's Dictionary*, Accountability is "an obligation or willingness to accept responsibility for one's actions."

A more developed description of Accountability can be found in the book *The OZ Principle*, by Conners, Smith and Hickman. *The **OZ Principle*** describes Accountability as "A personal choice to rise above one's circumstances and demonstrate the ownership necessary for achieving desired results – to See It, Own It, Solve It and Do It."

But what about Leadership Accountability? As Leaders, aren't we also Accountable for those we lead and the outcomes of their efforts? Within the book *Crucial Accountability*, the authors, Patterson, Grenny, Maxfield, McMillan and Switzler, discuss the Social Psychological term for which their book is named, Crucial Accountability.

Crucial Accountability describes the Accountability shared by all those involved in a situation, but rarely exercised. Examples can be as passive as people rudely cutting into lines ahead of others who choose to say nothing. Examples can also center around circumstances resulting in death and destruction because no one exercised Accountability to step up and identify a danger.

Remember the world watching the space shuttle Challenger breaking into pieces while in flight? It was later reported several engineers were concerned that some of the O-rings might fail, but withheld their opinions. People died and a nation was plunged into sadness.

Crucial Accountability represents those instances where an effective intervention is necessary to prevent the situation from going bad, or encourage the situation to improve.

Who are you as you lead?

LEADER'S STYLE MODEL

1. Accountable

2. Determined

THE RCA OF A
BALANCED LEADER

Are you a Determined Leader?

Are you decisive, purposeful, resolute and firmly resolved? When you decide to do something, do you determine that you will not allow anyone or anything to stop you or prevent you from reaching your goal?

Do you design your life to have substance? Is their intent behind your actions?

Do you keep going despite the barriers? Do you try one more time than the times you failed?

Vince Lombardi once said, "The price of success is hard work, dedication to the job at hand, and the determination that whether we win or lose, we have applied the best of ourselves to the task at hand."

Robert Hughes one said, "A determined soul will do more with a rusty monkey wrench than a loafer will accomplish with all the tools in a machine shop."

Who are you as you lead?

LEADER'S STYLE MODEL

1. Accountable

2. Determined

3. Assertive

THE RCA OF A
BALANCED LEADER

Are you an Assertive Leader?

Are you confident in your behavior? Are you enterprising and ambitious? Are you often described as a go-getter?

Assertive behavior is often confused with aggressive behavior; however, assertion does not involve hurting the other person either physically or emotionally.

If you are Assertive with others, you open the door for them to become Assertive in return thus improving productivity by leaps and bounds.

THE RCA OF A BALANCED LEADER

Who are you as you lead?

LEADER'S STYLE MODEL

1. Accountable

2. Determined

3. Assertive

4. Encouraging

THE RCA OF A BALANCED LEADER

Are you an Encouraging Leader?

Are you optimistic and upbeat? When you get involved with a project, do you bring a hopeful feeling to the table?

There are times when an Encouraging leader needs to offer criticism to be fair to those being led. Remember the words of Frank A. Clark who said, "Criticism, like rain, should be gentle enough to nourish a man's growth without destroying his roots."

By being an Encouraging leader, you are giving to those you lead.

Ralph Waldo Emerson once said, "The purpose of life is not to be happy. It is to be useful, to be honorable, to be compassionate, to have it make some difference that you have lived and lived well."

Martin Luther King Jr. once said, "Life's most urgent question is: What are you doing for others?"

Who are you as you lead?

LEADER'S STYLE MODEL

1. Accountable

2. Determined

3. Assertive

4. Encouraging

5. Persuasive

THE RCA OF A BALANCED LEADER

Are you a Persuasive Leader?

Are you able to guide people to do something or to believe in something of your choosing?Do you see yourself as compelling, convincing, effective and strong?

In order to persuade others, you have to believe in the project at hand yourself.

Thomas Carlyle once said "Let one who wants to move and convince others first be convinced and moved themselves."

So remember the proverb that tells us when a heart is filled with passion and is on fire, sparks will fly out of the mouth.

THE RCA OF A BALANCED LEADER

Who are you as you lead?

LEADER'S STYLE MODEL

1. Accountable

2. Determined

3. Assertive

4. Encouraging

5. Persuasive

6. Easy Going

THE RCA OF A BALANCED LEADER

Are you an Easy Going Leader?

Do you see your style and manner as relaxed and casual in your approach to those you lead? Do you think you are seen as happy-go-lucky and maybe laidback?

But, to quote that wise philosopher, Will Smith, "Don't confuse nice for soft."

You can be polite and respectful, giving the appearance of Easy Going, even in the worst of situations.

THE RCA OF A BALANCED LEADER

Who are you as you lead?

LEADER'S STYLE MODEL

1. Accountable

2. Determined

3. Assertive

4. Encouraging

5. Persuasive

6. Easy Going

7. Peacemaker

THE RCA OF A
BALANCED LEADER

Are you a Peacemaker type of Leader?

Do you work to prevent or stop arguments by being a go-between or mediator?

Peggy Haymes tells us in her book *Strugglers, Stragglers and Seekers,* "Avoiding conflict isn't peacemaking. Avoiding conflict means running away from the mess while peacemaking means running into the middle of it. Peacemaking means addressing those issues that caused conflict in the first place. Peacemaking means speaking the truth in love, but speaking the truth nonetheless."

Leader's Style Model

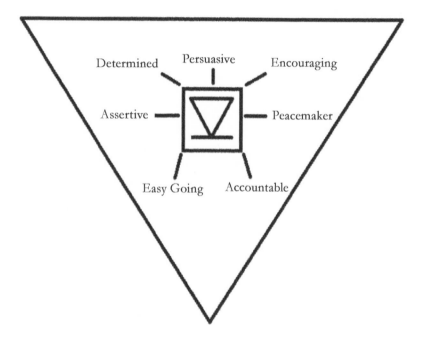

THE RCA OF A BALANCED LEADER

Leader's Style Model

Who in their right mind (or left mind as it were) could logically consider that a successful Leader could predominantly exhibit only one of these styles of Leadership? The true Leader must decide which of these styles is best suited for the task or people related to that current situation.

Also, stay aware of the probability that you are better at performing some of these leadership styles than you are at performing others. There are some styles you are so comfortable with they appear to be your areas of expertise.

On the other hand, you cannot pretend to be something you are not. For example, if you are a non-clinician, you should not pretend to be a Registered Nurse or a Physician.

During your analysis, stay aware of the possibility that you may believe you are exhibiting a specific management style, while others are seeing something else. Further question yourself; do others define your current management style with the same perception as you are defining yourself?

Additional situations will often require the Successful Leader to employ one or more of the other styles to achieve the new set of desired goals. Practice those styles that are not your strengths to earn a more comfortable exercise of those traits.

A successful golfer has more than one club in their bag.

THE RCA OF A BALANCED LEADER

Who they are often depends on who you are

RELFECTION MODEL

Reflection Model

Who they are often depends on who you are.

This one is powerful and fully with-in your control as a Leader. If you attach your assumptions to those you lead, you may be leading who you think you're leading instead of who you're actually leading. Success would be almost accidental under these circumstances. The psychological theory of Projection addresses just that.

You know Who You Lead and you know Who You Are as you Lead; often, Who They Are depends upon Who You Are.

THE RCA OF A BALANCED LEADER

Who they are often depends on who you are

RELFECTION MODEL

1. Projection

THE RCA OF A BALANCED LEADER

Projection - The attribution of one's own ideas, feelings, or attributes to other people. You often lead based on your perception of who you think you're leading. Are you seeing them clearly? Are you projecting onto those you lead what you want to see?

Consider this. You meet with someone you are trying to learn about. If you do most, if not all of the talking, and barely let the other person speak, you may see that person as you see yourself. If you like yourself, you will like them. On the other hand, if you don't like yourself, you may not like this person either.

Here's a suggestion about this. If you are trying to learn about the other person, let them talk. There's more than one reason God made the ears and mouth differently. The mouth can shut, but the ears can't.

Who they are often depends on who you are

RELFECTION MODEL

1. Projection

2. Priming the pump

THE RCA OF A
BALANCED LEADER

Priming the pump

You often get out of people what you put into them.

It's often like priming an old style water pump used on the farms in the past. You had to pour a little water in the top of the pump to clear the air from the pipe and allow your pumping action to bring the water up from the well, through the pipe and out of the spout. If you put dirt in the top of the pipe, you would prevent yourself from getting the water you were after. If you wanted water, you had to prime the pump with water. You got out what you put in.

Who they are often depends on who you are

RELFECTION MODEL

1. Projection

2. Priming the pump

3. Helping others

THE RCA OF A
BALANCED LEADER

Helping others

Do you need their help to succeed?

Your chance to help them is paramount at this point. Helping others – there is no better exercise for the heart than reaching down and lifting someone else up. When you help someone climb a mountain, you'll find yourself conquering the summit as well.

I've heard it asked, "If you were arrested for helping others, would there be enough evidence to convict you?"

There is so much anger and retaliation in the world. This should not be the basis of our decision making. With that in mind, I suggest you try to employ the statement I heard once that the only people you should try to get even with are those who have helped you.

Who they are often depends on who you are

RELFECTION MODEL

1. Projection

2. Priming the pump

3. Helping others

4. False assumptions

THE RCA OF A BALANCED LEADER

False assumptions

Unfounded or false assumptions of those you lead will alter your opinion of who they are. Be careful of this one.

Don't decide based on what others may have reported to you about those you lead. Investigate and decide for yourself.

Test out your own first impressions. You may have been having a bad day yourself thus tainting your first impression of the person.

Reflection Model

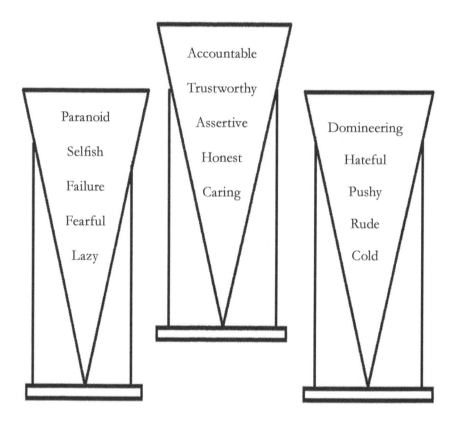

Paranoid
Selfish
Failure
Fearful
Lazy

Accountable
Trustworthy
Assertive
Honest
Caring

Domineering
Hateful
Pushy
Rude
Cold

Reflection Model

Remember the Michael Jackson song, *The Man in the Mirror*? How relevant that is for a Leader.

"If you want to make the world a better place

Take a look at yourself, and then make a change."

"OW!"

It all starts with you!

THE RCA OF A BALANCED LEADER

Who do you want to be as you lead?

Similarities?

THE RCA OF A BALANCED LEADER

Who do you want to be as you lead?

Similarities?

Who do you want to project? We exist on this Earth in one manner or another for many reasons. But in most cases, we can choose our manner. This can be a decidedly natural thing or it might be achieved through training, education, acclimation or emulation.

If you had to compare your particular manner or type to an animal, what would that animal be? Why would you choose that animal? Is it because of some trait you recognize in that animal or is it a trait you would like to emulate?

Here are a few animals whose traits I have seen in various individuals or groups. As you read this, ask yourself if you see any similarities to you or those around you.

Who do you want to be as you lead?

Similarities?

1. Squirrel

THE RCA OF A BALANCED LEADER

Squirrel

We've all seen squirrels in the wild. These animals exhibit a couple of traits worth mentioning. Have you watched squirrels as they go through their day? They cannot maintain focus.

They jump from one spot to another flipping their tails and jerking around in such a nervous manner they appear to never finish whatever they were working on. Let's not forget one of the squirrel's most distinctive characteristics – the manner in which they cross the road. They take on this major, possibly life-changing event with such uncertainty. They shoot out onto the road before they consider the possibility of danger. Suddenly they then appear to detect danger. This often occurs when they are more than half way across the road, almost to their goal. This is where their nature takes over. They become indecisive. They waiver and begin going back and forth over the surface of the road they have already crossed making no progress in any direction. Too often they make a snap decision, appearing to be made out of desperation, and dart back to their starting point crossing over all the road surface they had already traversed placing themselves in the clear path of monstrous traffic. Squirrels often suffer death by indecision.

Who do you want to be as you lead?

Similarities?

1. Squirrel

2. Opossum

THE RCA OF A BALANCED LEADER

Opossum

Then there is the not-so-often-seen Opossum. This critter strives to live outside the lime light. The Opossum often seeks to disassociate itself from others. It appears the Opossum believes that to stay to itself and ignore the world around it is its best approach to survival. Keep your head down, don't make waves, and maybe they'll not notice you. This is the way the Opossum believes best to go from day to day. The Opossum takes this as far as any creature can when finding itself out in the open with attention of the world drawn directly to it, it plays dead. Playing dead is the Opossum's way of holding on just one more day.

THE RCA OF A BALANCED LEADER

Who do you want to be as you lead?

Similarities?

1. Squirrel

2. Opossum

3. Buzzard

THE RCA OF A
BALANCED LEADER

Buzzard

What about Buzzards? They seem to live a fairly relaxed life. While other animals forage and build, the Buzzard sits and waits for disaster to arise. You see, the Buzzard flourishes when other animals die. The Buzzard survives by identifying a dead or dying animal and waiting until that animal has given up its fight. It doesn't produce or nurture. The Buzzard is a scavenger. A scavenger feeds on death. There are scavengers of all types. Buzzards prey upon the failure of others.

Who do you want to be as you lead?

Similarities?

1. Squirrel

2. Opossum

3. Buzzard

4. Honey Bee

THE RCA OF A BALANCED LEADER

Honey Bee

Being a fan of honey, I often consider the Honey Bees. They are busy and productive creatures. Their hives are usually well-formed and often so filled with the honey they produce they have plenty to share with we humans. Honey Bees appear to be very organized with the life and survival of the hive being their paramount goal. But what happens to the Honey Bee when the hive is affected by some overwhelmingly negative circumstance? I have personally witnessed hives when their Queen has been killed. The hive becomes an organic monster hell-bent on destruction. Each of the formerly productive Honey Bees takes on a surprisingly different persona of anger and destruction. These Honey Bees form a tightly packed ball in the air blaming each other for the problems of the hive. They continue this aerial assault until these Honey Bees have completely destroyed one another. Honey Bees may normally be productive, but when things get tough, they turn on each other.

Who do you want to be as you lead?

Similarities?

1. Squirrel

2. Opossum

3. Buzzard

4. Honey Bee

5. Lion

THE RCA OF A
BALANCED LEADER

Lion - No animal is perfect, but the image of the Lion is also one to consider. The Lion is an Apex Predator — at the top of their food chain with no real predators of their own. Highly distinctive, the Lion is depicted as strong, noble, brave, appearing to be of royalty and stateliness. Interestingly, the Lion is the most socially inclined of all wild cats. They most often reside in groups with a mixture of males, females and cubs. A Lion's family group is called a 'Pride.' The area they live in is called a 'Pride Area' and as Apex Predators, they have a crucial role in maintaining the health of their ecosystem, their Pride Area. As such, Lions take on the responsibility for their environment and the world around them. Each adult in the group has their own responsibilities of hunting, nurturing and protecting the group. Lions will hunt as individuals, but most often they hunt in coordinated groups to provide the best advantage for success and thus the livelihood of the Pride. Lions are bold, while still caring for one another. Lions are brave, yet loving to their Pride. Lions coordinate together for success, while remaining individuals.

Were there traits you recognized? Only a few of the attributes of each animal have been highlighted herein, but I bet you identified circumstances in your life and the lives of those around you where each animal lives. Which animal do you want to be likened to? It's a choice. It's your choice to assist those around you in becoming the animal you or they want to be.

Which of these animals and their traits do you want to project? Which of the animals and their traits do you feel will be beneficial to those you lead?

Again, who do you want to be as you lead?

Acquired Understanding Model

Who?

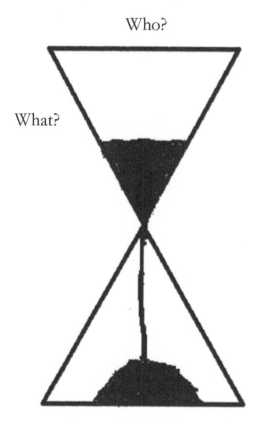

What?

THE RCA OF A BALANCED LEADER

Acquired Understanding Model - What?

THE RCA OF A BALANCED LEADER

WHAT?

What do you lead?

THE RCA OF A
BALANCED LEADER

What do you lead?

Within your work life, you may be responsible for one or more of the areas we are discussing. There are basics to keep in mind which are relevant to each of these areas. Let this be a cursory discussion of these areas that will open you to a deeper understanding of what you lead and what those around you lead.

THE RCA OF A BALANCED LEADER

WHAT?

What do you lead?

1. Department

THE RCA OF A BALANCED LEADER

Are you a Department Leader?

If you are, then you have departmental goals and expectations. You have a budget that includes labor and supplies for your department. You have overall expectations which are achieved by specific and successful efforts, which in turn produce desired outcomes.

As a Department Leader, you may have one or two staff members you lead or you may have dozens.

Your goals are finite – they are specific and measurable. If they are achieved, your department benefits the entire operation. As a Department Leader, you must make sure you understand your department's goals and work to align your team with those goals. You must determine if your department has the resources to achieve those goals and if not, what you must do to obtain those needed resources.

If your goals are not achieved, you have the responsibility of leading yourself and your line staff in the areas where they need the most assistance. You may do this by soliciting your department's feedback and constructive criticism.

You lead to achieve the level of success that has been set as your expected Standard of Performance.

WHAT?

What do you lead?

1. Department

2. Facility

THE RCA OF A
BALANCED LEADER

Are you a Facility Leader?

If you are, then you have multiple sets of departmental goals and expectations.

You have a budget that not only includes labor and supplies, but also bricks and mortar expenses to maintain the building structure and all of its related utilities. In addition to the expense side, as a Facility Leader you also have revenue goals and expectations.

As a Facility Leader, you will have multiple departments you lead most effectively through successful department leaders.

Many of your goals are finite, but not all of them. Measuring Customer Satisfaction, for instance, doesn't always produce finite outcomes and isn't always measured by finite methods. As a Facility Leader, you must make sure you understand your various department's goals and work to align your Department Leaders with those goals. You must determine if your various departments have the resources to achieve those goals and if not, what you must do to assist in obtaining those needed resources.

If your goals are not achieved, you have the responsibility of leading yourself, your Department Leaders, and sometimes assisting in leading the line staff in an area where the Department Leader needs assistance.

You lead to achieve the level of success that has been set as your expected Standard of Performance.

THE RCA OF A BALANCED LEADER

WHAT?

What do you lead?

1. Department

2. Facility

3. Region

Are you a Region Leader?

If you are, then you have multiple sets of facility goals and expectations.

You have budgets that include expenses, labor, revenue, bricks and mortar costs, capital expenses purchases and net income calculations. You also share the HR responsibilities that go along with leading a few hundred individuals.

As a Region Leader, you will have multiple facilities you lead, most effectively through the Facility Leaders. Also as a Region Leader, you share a responsibility for not only the success of your Facility Leaders, but also the success of their individual Department Leaders.

If your goals are not achieved, you have the responsibility of leading yourself, your Facility Leaders, and sometimes assisting in leading front line staff.

You lead to achieve the level of success that has been set as your expected Standard of Performance.

WHAT?

What do you lead?

1. Department

2. Facility

3. Region

4. State

Are you a State Leader?

If you are, then you have multiple sets of regional goals and expectations.

You have budgets that include expenses, labor, revenue, bricks and mortar, capital expense purchases, net income calculations, and the coordination and cost of a state-wide supporting staff. This state-wide staff provides the off and on site services and guidance necessary to pursue success and achieve the established goals and expectations.

If you goals are not achieved, you have the responsibility of leading yourself, your Regional Leaders, their Facility Leaders, their Department Leaders, and sometimes assisting in leading the front line staff.

You lead to achieve the level of success that has been set as your expected Standard of Performance.

WHAT?

What do you lead?

1. Department

2. Facility

3. Region

4. State

5. Company

THE RCA OF A BALANCED LEADER

Are you a Company Leader?

Let's cut to the chase - it's all on your plate.

How are you evaluating yourself in this role?
What are your checks and balances?

You Lead to Achieve.

WHAT?

What do you lead?

1. Department

2. Facility

3. Region

4. State

5. Company

6. People – people are the trees that make up your forest

THE RCA OF A
BALANCED LEADER

You've heard the phrase, "you can't see the Forest for the Trees."

People are the trees that make up your Forest. No matter what level you lead, People - this is the only real answer.

Budgets, goals, expectations - only achieved through People.

Department, Facility, Region, State, Company - all made up of People.

People are the trees that make up your Forest.

You Lead People to Achieve!

What are the goals of those you lead?

THE RCA OF A
BALANCED LEADER

What are the goals of those you lead?

To examine the goals of those we lead, let's consider Maslow's Hierarchy of Needs.

Maslow wanted to understand what motivates people. He believed that people possess a set of motivation systems unrelated to rewards or unconscious desires. Maslow stated that people are motivated to achieve certain needs. When one need is fulfilled a person seeks to fulfill the next one and so on. The most widespread version of Maslow's hierarchy of needs includes five motivational needs which can be divided into basic needs - physiological, safety, love, esteem, and growth needs represented as self-actualization.

The basic needs are said to motivate people when the needs are unmet. Also, the need to fulfil such needs will become stronger the longer the duration they are denied. For example, the longer a person goes without food the more hungry they will become.

One must satisfy lower level basic needs before progressing on to meet higher level growth needs. Once these needs have been reasonably satisfied, one may be able to reach the highest level called self-actualization.

What are the goals of those you lead?

Maslow's Hierarchy of Needs

Maslow's Hierarchy of Needs five-stage model includes:

1. Biological and Physiological needs - air, food, drink, shelter, warmth, sex, sleep.

2. Safety needs - protection from elements, security, order, law, stability, freedom from fear.

3. Love and belongingness needs - friendship, intimacy, affection and love, - from work group, family, friends, and romantic relationships.

4. Esteem needs - achievement, mastery, independence, status, dominance, prestige, self-respect, and respect from others.

5. Self-Actualization needs - realizing personal potential, self-fulfillment, seeking personal growth and peak experiences.

What are the goals of those you lead?

1. Paycheck

THE RCA OF A BALANCED LEADER

What are the goals of those you lead?

Paycheck

A lot of our people live from check to check. Without a paycheck, one single paycheck, they would fall behind. This is a major focus.

This certainly may be placed at Maslow's first level of basic needs – Biological and Physiological needs - air, food, drink, shelter, warmth, sex, sleep.

THE RCA OF A BALANCED LEADER

What are the goals of those you lead?

1. Paycheck

2. Food, Home, Car

THE RCA OF A BALANCED LEADER

What are the goals of those you lead?

Food, Home, Car

These also fit within Maslow's first level of Biological and Physiological needs - air, food, drink, shelter, warmth, sex, sleep.

THE RCA OF A BALANCED LEADER

What are the goals of those you lead?

1. Paycheck

2. Food, Home, Car

3. Taking care of their families by working

THE RCA OF A BALANCED LEADER

What are the goals of those you lead?

Taking care of their families, in part by working.

Providing for their Safety needs - protection from the elements, security, order, law, stability, freedom from fear.

Personal and financial security, including things like health and life insurance would fit here at this level.

Love and belongingness needs are often addressed at this level as well - friendship, intimacy, affection and love, - from work group, family, friends, and romantic relationships.

What are the goals of those you lead?

1. Paycheck

2. Food, Home, Car

3. Taking care of their families by working

4. Obtain a level of success and achieve a sense of value from their efforts

THE RCA OF A BALANCED LEADER

What are the goals of those you lead?

Obtaining a level of success can be viewed at Maslow's basic level to satisfy the Esteem needs - achievement, mastery, independence, status, dominance, prestige, self-respect, and respect from others.

This is a level where people feel accepted and valued by others as a result of their own achievements.

THE RCA OF A BALANCED LEADER

What drives you?

THE RCA OF A
BALANCED LEADER

What drives you?

If we use Maslow's Hierarchy of Needs, we could logically assume that even if we have not mastered Maslow's first three levels of Physiological/Biological, Safety and Love/Belonging needs, most of us are living most often at Maslow's Esteem level.

With this in mind, even if as Maslow stated we are still working on the first three levels from time to time, we are most often driven by accomplishments which nurture our self- esteem.

So as Leaders, what drives you to achieve?

What drives you?

1. We fuel our creativity by those which we choose to surround ourselves

THE RCA OF A BALANCED LEADER

What drives you? We fuel our creativity by those which we choose to surround ourselves. Who do you associate with?

If you surround yourself with creative, energetic people, the chances are much higher you will be more creative and energetic as well.

Ever play tennis or racquetball with someone who plays a little better than you? You learn, you grow; you start playing a little better.

Ever see a really good football or basketball team play against another team that is not as good? Sometimes, the better team starts slacking off and not play as well – nearly, or in fact completely, losing the game to the less talented team. They played down to the level of the inferior team.

There's a farming term – being equally yoked. If you have two horses pulling a wagon or a plow who are equally strong and share the same temperament, then the process of pulling will go smoothly and effectively. If one of the horses is stronger than the other, or if one of the horses is jumpy and lacks the ability to concentrate on the task at hand, the process of pulling will be hindered and possibly destroyed by these differences.

All relationships could be compared to these dynamics.

What drives you?

1. We fuel our creativity by those which we choose to surround ourselves

2. Do you Drive yourself or are you Driven by others?

THE RCA OF A
BALANCED LEADER

What drives you?

Do you drive yourself or are you driven by others?

Picture an open range of land covered with grassy fields. Moving across those fields is a large herd of cattle being moved from one location to another.

Now picture a Cowboy on horseback whose responsibility it is to move those cattle to the new location. The Cowboy is riding the horse and driving the herd of cattle where he chooses.

Are you Riding or are you being Ridden? Are you Driving or are you being Driven?

THE RCA OF A BALANCED LEADER

What drives you?

1. We fuel our creativity by those which we choose to surround ourselves

2. Do you Drive yourself or are you Driven by others?

3. Are you open or closed to being Driven by others?

THE RCA OF A BALANCED LEADER

What drives you?

Are you open or closed to being Driven by others?

As leaders, we all have someone whose goal it is to lead us. The Cowboy has a Trail Boss. The Trail Boss has a Ranch Manager. The Ranch Manager has a Ranch Owner, and so on.

Being effectively driven by those who lead us is often essential to our success. Effectively, and appropriately, driving those we lead is also quite essential to not only their success, but ours as well.

The Cowboy would be ineffective without the horse. The horse provides strength, courage, patience and the ability for the Cowboy to properly position himself to lead as the needs of the herd change.

THE RCA OF A BALANCED LEADER

What drives you?

1. We fuel our creativity by those which we choose to surround ourselves

2. Do you Drive yourself or are you Driven by others?

3. Are you open or closed to being Driven by others?

4. Do you acclimate or do you alter your circumstances / surroundings?

THE RCA OF A
BALANCED LEADER

What drives you?

Do you acclimate or do you alter your circumstances / surroundings?

This should be a case-by-case decision. Assessing what is already in place helps with this determination.

There are those though who cannot build on someone else's work and must start on their own. There are also those who cannot start with nothing and build something – they must have the foundation initiated by another.

What holds you back?

THE RCA OF A BALANCED LEADER

What holds you back?

Fear – <u>F</u>alse <u>E</u>vidence <u>A</u>ppearing <u>R</u>eal

How we manage our insecurities is very important.

In Social Psychology, there are two dynamics divided by a clear distinction of reality. These two dynamics are called "High Anxiety" and "Low Anxiety." The words High and Low have nothing to do with the amount or level of anxiety. They are merely labels to separate these dynamics on a comparative scale.

High Anxiety is like having a bear in your face – the reality of something of credible existence to fear.

Low Anxiety is like thinking there might be a bear around the corner. You don't see or hear the bear – you have no proof of the bear's existence.

It is the Low Anxiety that will tear you up – the overwhelming worry with nothing factual to set as your target. Literally, worrying yourself to death over a maybe or a might be.

What holds you back?

1. Fear Cripples

Fear Cripples

If you allow fear to take hold, it prevents you from moving forward, it cripples you. But every obstacle you encounter further introduces you to your true self. When you learn more about yourself in this process you become stronger and better prepared for the next issue.

Do remember, no one is immune to problems. Even the Lion has to fight off flies.

THE RCA OF A BALANCED LEADER

What holds you back?

1. Fear Cripples

2. Your fear of the short term can blind you to long term success

THE RCA OF A BALANCED LEADER

Your fear of the short term can blind you to long term success.

The short term — a small thing in itself, but usually a segue to something greater.

Why was it such a big deal for Neil Armstrong to take that first step off the ladder onto the surface of the Moon? "A small step for man" represented the conquering of one tremendous long term goal, as well as the beginning of a new set of long term goals.

That short step, albeit a transitional action, was also a short term goal. Take the step or not? This may seem to be an easy decision from our current point of view, but that decision has already been made. Today is after the fact. We are not faced with that decision at this moment.

We are faced with short term decisions daily. We all respond to those differently and how we respond to the short term decisions will dictate how we succeed with our long term goals.

What holds you back?

1. Fear Cripples

2. Your fear of the short term can blind you to long term success

3. Often, people respond based on insecurities. What if people responded based on their strengths?

THE RCA OF A BALANCED LEADER

Often people respond / plan based on their various insecurities.

Insecurities are imbedded throughout our decision making systems. With some people, those insecurities strongly effect their decision making. With others, those insecurities have been resolved or are kept in check. Either way, overcoming them through practice creates a place of strength that replaces weakness.

The worst thing to do is to give in to the insecurity, the fear, and do nothing. No one succeeds all the time; but, you don't want to miss an opportunity as a result of fear.

Courage and success don't exist because of a lack of fear – it is performing admirably in the face of fear that exemplifies courage and success.

How would relationships / circumstances be different if people responded based on their strengths?

What holds you back?

1. Fear Cripples

2. Your fear of the short term can blind you to long term success

3. Often, people respond based on insecurities. What if people responded based on their strengths?

4. "Sometimes you win, sometimes you lose; and most times you choose between the two —"

THE RCA OF A BALANCED LEADER

In the words of Carole King, in her song *Sweet Seasons*,

"Sometimes you win; sometimes you lose;
And most times you choose between the two –
Wonderin' – wonderin' if you have made it.

Sure does appeal to me;
You know we can get there easily –
Just like a sail boat a-sailin' on the sea."

THE RCA OF A
BALANCED LEADER

What holds you back?

1. In life, as on the raging sea, when the winds threaten to knock you off your course or capsize you entirely, don't turn away – Keep Facin' It!

THE RCA OF A BALANCED LEADER

In life, as on the raging sea, when the winds threaten to knock you off your course or capsize you entirely, don't turn away – Keep Facin' It!

Your boat is sailing on the sea. Waves of all size are on the sea.

To run parallel with the waves shows the waves your weak side. To run parallel with the waves is an attempt to ignore them – thinking they may dissipate and go away.

To hit the waves head on is showing the waves your strong side – it's attacking the issue from your strengths.

The only way a boat will survive is by hitting the waves head on! Otherwise, the boat will rollover and capsize.

When you encounter strong waves, strong winds – hit them head on! Don't look back and don't be sidelined by your fear. Remember, you're the Leader.

Keep Facin' It!

THE RCA OF A BALANCED LEADER

What holds you back?

1. In life, as on the raging sea, when the winds threaten to knock you off your course or capsize you entirely, don't turn away – Keep Facin' It!

2. "Suffer just enough to sing the blues"

THE RCA OF A BALANCED LEADER

"Suffer just enough to sing the blues"

Remember the words of an Elton John song, "Suffer just enough to sing the blues." You need to be bothered or concerned enough to do something about it – not so much as to stifle your efforts.

Don't deny or ignore the pain – the difficulty.   Pain is real; difficulty is real; obstacles exist.

To "suffer just enough to sing the blues" is to recognize the pain – the difficulty, and respond productively to it and not run from it!

Remember the military mantra concerning addressing obstacles: Over, Under, Around or Through!

Go Over it!
Go Under it!
Go Around it!
Or
Go Through it!

Acquired Understanding Model

Who?

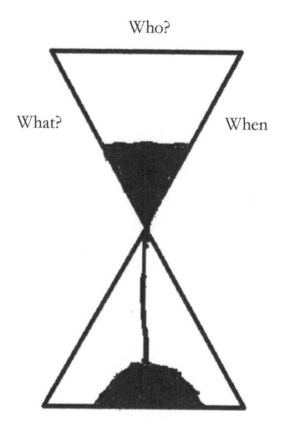

What?

When

THE RCA OF A
BALANCED LEADER

Acquired Understanding Model - When?

When?

When are you a Leader?

THE RCA OF A
BALANCED LEADER

When are you a Leader?

Whether you are aware of it or not, chances are that throughout the week you lead in more than one arena.

THE RCA OF A BALANCED LEADER

When?

When are you a Leader?

1. Home

THE RCA OF A BALANCED LEADER

Home

If you're a parent, you're a Leader at home.

Your Leadership skills as a parent get tested from time to time. Sometimes with monumental issues – sometimes with issues that are important, but not at the life threatening level.

But never forget the effect you have on your home as you exercise your Leadership role in your home.

When?

When are you a Leader?

1. Home

2. Work

THE RCA OF A BALANCED LEADER

Work

Are you a Leader at work?

Well, if you don't think you're a Leader at Work, you need to start this presentation / book all over again from page one.

When?

When are you a Leader?

1. Home

2. Work

3. Community

Community

Are you a Leader in your community?

Are you a part of any service clubs?

Are you a part of a Faith-based group?

Are you a part of a Neighborhood association?

Are you a part of your Children's school?

Are you a part of a Secret Vigilantly group that fights crime one criminal at a time?

THE RCA OF A BALANCED LEADER

When do you lead and then when do
you step aside and let others lead?

THE RCA OF A
BALANCED LEADER

When do you lead and then when do you step aside and let others lead?

There are those times, those situations, when you are not the Leader. You obviously lead, but some particular or specific circumstances present themselves creating an opportunity for Leadership within which you are not the Leader.

THE RCA OF A
BALANCED LEADER

When do you lead and then when do
you step aside and let others lead?

1. How do you determine?

THE RCA OF A BALANCED LEADER

How do you determine?

If there is more than one Leader available for the project, you have the opportunity to discern which is best suited to lead in that situation. It's a case by case decision.

Examination of the circumstances – sometimes quickly; sometimes through the planning stages – is a must to determine which Leader should be in charge.

One such example comes to mind. I was paged "STAT" to the back hallway of the building in which I was the Administrator. I hurried there to find a group of staff members gathered around the building's van driver who was lying on his back, on the floor.

People were making comments of what should be done. I pushed through, asked what happened, and discovered he was found sitting in a chair near his current position, slouched and non-responsive. For fear of his falling from the chair, the staff had lowered him to the floor where he now rested.

I got on the floor next to the man, I lifted his head off the floor and held it gently but firmly off the floor. I looked up to the Director of Nursing – the Chief Medical staff member in the group – and firmly told her "You are in charge! You tell us what to do!" Everyone else shut up and the Director

of Nursing began handing out instructions. I made one Leadership decision by placing whom I determined was the best person for the task at hand in control. S h e spoke and we followed.

When do you lead and then when do you step aside and let others lead?

1. How do you determine?

2. How hard is it for you to step aside?

THE RCA OF A BALANCED LEADER

How hard is it for you to step aside?

Ego? Do you think you're the only one who can do the job, complete the task, correctly? Does it seem easier to just do it yourself rather than assign, teach and implement; thus delegating the task to someone you lead?

Remember President John Kennedy's Peace Corp lesson? It went something like, give a man fish and he'll eat today. Teach him to fish and he'll eat for the rest of his life.

Concern? Do you have a concern about the skills, abilities or knowledge level of those you lead? Will this ever change if you continue to do their job for them?

When do you lead and then when do
you step aside and let others lead?

1. How do you determine?

2. How hard is it for you to step aside?

3. My Management Role Model – Captain James T. Kirk

THE RCA OF A
BALANCED LEADER

My management Role Model is Captain James T. Kirk of the Starship Enterprise.

I know it sounds like comedy, but let me explain.

Kirk would go into a situation not knowing enough about it to make a good decision. But Kirk did know how to surround himself with the best and most talented people.

He knew how to coordinate those people.

Kirk knew how to get out of their way and let them get their jobs done.

And Kirk learned about this situation through the process. On the days when this model is a success – those are good days!

Acquired Understanding Model

Who?

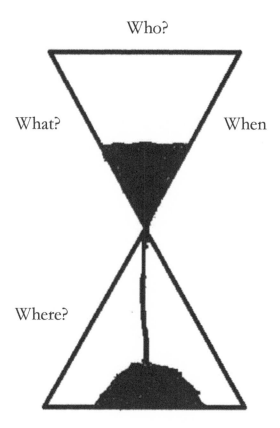

What?   When

Where?

Acquired Understanding Model - Where?

Where is the best place to lead them?

THE RCA OF A BALANCED LEADER

Where is the best place to lead them?

Wow, you're a Leader and you're surrounded by people ready to be led. Where do you lead them?

This is arguably one of the more important questions to ask yourself. If people seem to be drawn to the direction you choose to move, you bare a great responsibility for where they wind up.

I'm sure that many times have you have heard a popular sports or entertainment figure, with obvious talent, living in what appears to be a successful achievement of the goals they set out to attain, voice firmly, "I am not anyone's Role Model." We have heard this all too often, in my opinion.

People look to those who achieve to follow and to emulate. These people are Leaders. Role Models are Leaders, whether they choose to be or not. Their attained position alone set them up as Leaders. We too, if for no other reason the positions we have attained, are Leaders who are followed in part because of those attained positions.

Consider the analogy that we as Leaders pour gasoline on a fire. We highlight and possibly amplify what we become involved with. It is our responsibility to gauge and measure how much gasoline we pour on those fires and when.

We must choose our fires and decide how much fuel we apply – but our mere presence effects the fire. We must determine where to lead.

THE RCA OF A BALANCED LEADER

Where is the best place to lead them?

1. How do you decide?

THE RCA OF A
BALANCED LEADER

How do you decide?

If you are solely, or nearly such, responsible for determining where you are to lead the team, you need to start at ground level. What is the purpose of your entity? How should your position or involvement effect that purpose? What benefit can the efforts of your team bring to the purpose of your entity? What are the best efforts / results your team could bring to bear?

These questions could help you to determine where to lead your team.

THE RCA OF A BALANCED LEADER

Where is the best place to lead them?

1. How do you decide?

2. Mutually establishing goals

THE RCA OF A BALANCED LEADER

Mutually establishing goals

If the desired results are already determined and set out for your entity, then you need to get with your team to determine mutually established goals designed to achieve those results.

Discussion and exchange between you, the Leader, and your team, those you lead, in this situation sets and accepts those goals. It should then become clear to you where to lead you team to achieve those goals.

Acquired Understanding Model

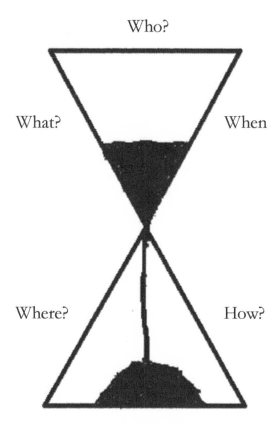

Who?

What?   When

Where?   How?

THE RCA OF A
BALANCED LEADER

Acquired Understanding Model - How?

How?

How do you lead?

1. Do as I do – Example

THE RCA OF A BALANCED LEADER

Do as I do – Example

Do you lead by example? Are you one who physically shows those you lead how to perform their task at hand?

Do you act and react in a manner that is exampling how you want those you lead to act and react?

Do you speak to others in a manner that is exampling how you want those you lead to speak to others?

Do you treat others in a manner that is exampling how you want those you lead to treat others?

How?

How do you lead?

1. Do as I do – Example

2. Do as I say – Instruct

THE RCA OF A
BALANCED LEADER

Do as I say – Instruct

Maybe you don't always have an overt opportunity to example the behaviors you expect out of those you lead.

Since you may not have the opportunity to example the behaviors of how you want those you lead to act, react, speak to and treat others, you choose to instruct those you lead on you expectations in these areas.

If this is your manner of leading, make sure you stay true to your own instruction if and when an opportunity to example your behavior arises.

To instruct with one set of expectations and then example behaviors in conflict with those instructed expectations will generate confusion.

THE RCA OF A BALANCED LEADER

How?

How do you lead?

1. Do as I do – Example

2. Do as I say – Instruct

3. Don't do as I do, do as I say - Confusion

THE RCA OF A BALANCED LEADER

Don't do as I do, do as I say – Confusion

This dynamic creates a potential for many negative results. And don't try to fool yourself, they are results – something that is generated or exists because of the actions of something else.

What a shame if that something else is a direct result of confusion caused by your actions or lack of action.

Let's examine one such resulting negative dynamic.

THE RCA OF A BALANCED LEADER

The Disconnect

THE RCA OF A
BALANCED LEADER

The Disconnect - Be careful of a major pitfall in how you lead.

If two key managers / departments are not effectively communicating, at the very least they are non-productive. This breakdown may in fact become destructive.

If leadership is not effectively communicating with the line staff, again, at the very least this would be non-productive. This particular breakdown may in fact become extremely destructive.

We can't manage silence!

The Disconnect

1. There is Disaster in the Disconnect

There is Disaster in the Disconnect

The Head is no longer in communication with the Body

The Head is not aware of the disconnect

Trust begins to diminish during a disconnect

The Disconnect

1. There is Disaster in the Disconnect

2. There is death in the Disconnect

THE RCA OF A BALANCED LEADER

There is Death in the Disconnect.

How many relationships break-up claiming they grew apart, they grew in different directions – they Disconnected!

The Disconnect

1. There is Disaster in the Disconnect

2. There is death in the Disconnect

3. Active communication prevents the Disconnect

Active communication prevents The Disconnect

You must be approachable.

You must be trustworthy.

You must be concerned about their lives.

You must be concerned about their challenges.

The Disconnect

1. There is Disaster in the Disconnect

2. There is death in the Disconnect

3. Active communication prevents the Disconnect

4. If they don't talk with you, they will talk with someone

If they don't talk with you, they will talk with someone

Resign and talk with a new employer.

Talk with each other causing a festering problem and increased separation.

Talk with your customers causing a broadened Disconnect.

Talk with regulatory agencies, causing Dante's Inferno.

Acquired Understanding Model

Who?

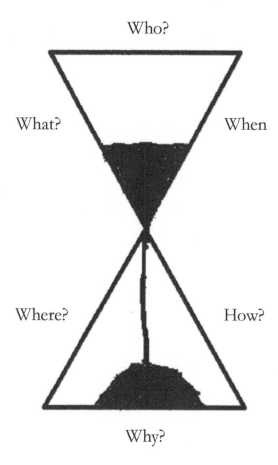

What?   When

Where?   How?

Why?

THE RCA OF A
BALANCED LEADER

Acquired Understanding Model - Why?

Why?

Why do you lead?

THE RCA OF A BALANCED LEADER

Why do you lead?

I've heard it said many times that there are two very important days in your life.

1 – The day you were born.

2 – The day you discover Why you were born.

"Why" you were born may or may not perfectly match "why" you lead. But rest assured, they are linked. If you were born to lead others, then who, what, when, where and how you lead becomes even more relevant. If you were born to achieve a different goal, for a different reason, then leading others may be the vehicle you use to achieve that different goal.

"Why" you lead is an important question.

Nietzsche says, "He who has a why to live for can bear almost any how."

Why?

Why do you lead?

1. What do you get out of leading? A sense of...?

THE RCA OF A BALANCED LEADER

What do you get out of leading? A sense of…?

Do you Lead to Achieve?

Are you trying to satisfy your need for esteem, mastery, status, self-respect, or gain respect from others?

Do you like the view from the front of the pack?

Do you like pushing down buttons, rather than the feeling of pushing up daisies?

Why?

Why do you lead?

1. What do you get out of leading? A sense of…?

2. Today is brand new, never been used – Make the most of it!

THE RCA OF A BALANCED LEADER

Today is brand new, never been used – Make the most of it!

So don't be stopped by history; by whatever happened yesterday. Build on it and use it as a foundation for a better tomorrow.

Be more like the Tea Kettle than the squeaky wheel – A tea kettle is up to its neck in hot water and is still singing.

A squeaky wheel gets the grease, but the squeakiest wheel usually gets replaced!

Complaining about a situation will not help you understand Why you Lead. Identifying the failings of the circumstance or the system and attacking or assisting in the attack designed to remedy the failings, predicated by the way you go about that task – that attack, may make it crystal clear Why you Lead.

Today is brand new, never been used – Make the most of it!

Balanced Leader Model

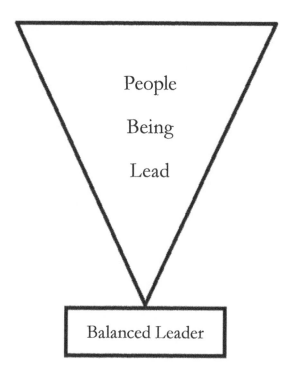

People

Being

Lead

Balanced Leader

THE RCA OF A
BALANCED LEADER

A Balanced Leader is at the pinnacle of the pyramid; but, the pyramid is inverted. A Balanced Leader balances out the efforts, abilities, attributes and goals of all those they lead. This is achieved through Acquired Understanding.

A Balanced Leader is at the pinnacle of the pyramid; but the pyramid is inverted!

1. Personal Growth Model

Personal Growth Model

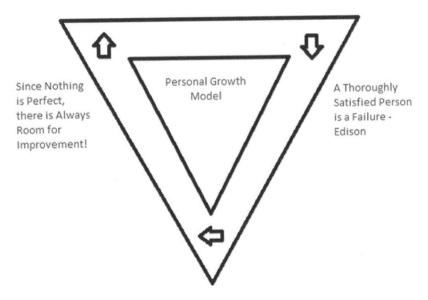

The Unexamined Life is not Worth Living - Socrates

Personal Growth Model

Since Nothing is Perfect, there is Always Room for Improvement!

A Thoroughly Satisfied Person is a Failure - Edison

A Balanced Leader is at the pinnacle of the
pyramid; but the pyramid is inverted!

1. Personal Growth Model

2. Success Model

Success Model

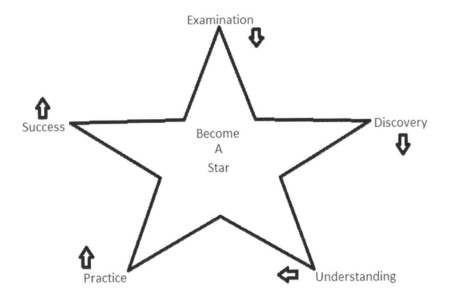

THE RCA OF A BALANCED LEADER

A Balanced Leader is at the pinnacle of the pyramid; but the pyramid is inverted!

1. Personal Growth Model

2. Success Model

3. Acquired Understanding Model

Acquired Understanding Model

Who?

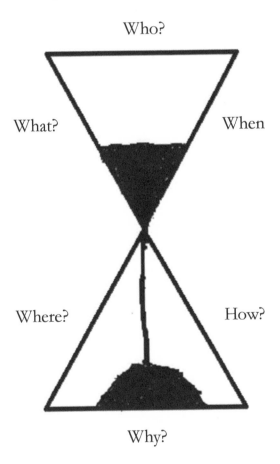

What?

When

Where?

How?

Why?

THE RCA OF A BALANCED LEADER

A Balanced Leader is at the pinnacle of the pyramid; but the pyramid is inverted!

1. Personal Growth Model

2. Success Model

3. Acquired Understanding Model

4. Shared Goals Model

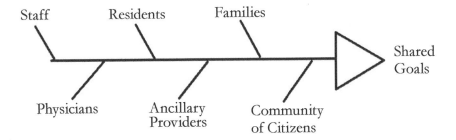

Staff Residents Families

Shared
Goals

Physicians Ancillary
Providers Community
of Citizens

A Balanced Leader is at the pinnacle of the pyramid; but the pyramid is inverted!

1. Personal Growth Model

2. Success Model

3. Acquired Understanding Model

4. Shared Goals Model

5. Leader's Style Model

Leader's Style Model

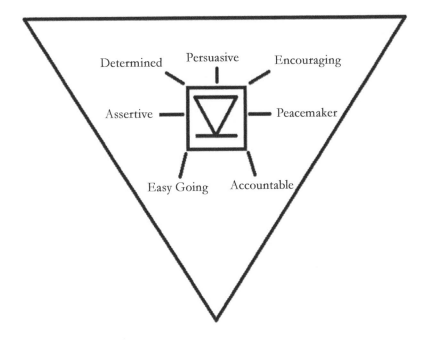

A Balanced Leader is at the pinnacle of the pyramid; but the pyramid is inverted!

1. Personal Growth Model

2. Success Model

3. Acquired Understanding Model

4. Shared Goals Model

5. Leader's Style Model

6. Reflection Model

Reflection Model

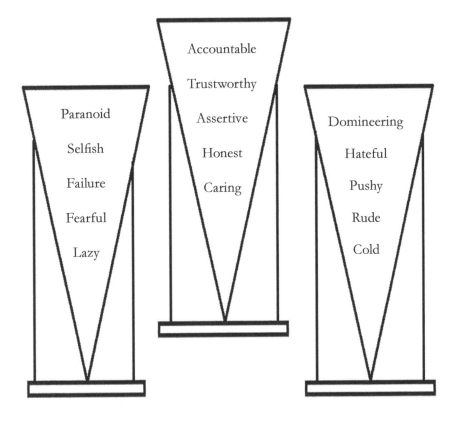

THE RCA OF A BALANCED LEADER

A Balanced Leader is at the pinnacle of the pyramid; but the pyramid is inverted!

1. Personal Growth Model

2. Success Model

3. Acquired Understanding Model

4. Shared Goals Model

5. Leader's Style Model

6. Reflection Model

7. Balanced Leader Model

Balanced Leader Model

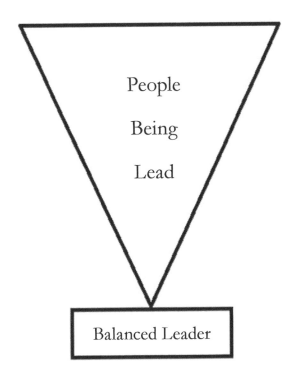

People

Being

Lead

Balanced Leader

About the Authors

Phil Ford has been immersed in leadership roles from a young age. Although education and experience have molded many of Ford's modes of operation, he attributes the bulk of his earned wisdom to great teachers and enlightened mentors. Among his leadership roles throughout his career, Ford has successfully served as president and vice president for many of the entities with which he has partnered.

Michael Blisko has worked his way to the top of various organizational hierarchies. Michael started as a frontline worker eager to grow. His successful growth through the ranks has been further nurtured by the experiences gained through his educational achievements. Michael serves as principal and chief executive officer of various health care organizations and has served by either chairing or holding seats on numerous boards of directors for other health care organizations.